A Portrait of

WEST VIRGINIA

Arnout Hyde, Jr.

CONTENTS

Published by QUARRIER PRESS
4th Printing 1997

Printed and bound in Hong Kong by Everbest printing Co., Ltd.

Page 1—A STONE FORMATION RESEMBLING A FACE IN FAYETTE COUNTY.
Overleaf—SUMMER MORNING MIST LINGERS OVER ROUTE 32 NEAR HARMON.
Opposite Page—FOG ENSHROUDS MOUNTAINS IN BOONE COUNTY.

This book may be ordered through:

Quarrier Press
1416 Quarrier Street
Charleston, West Virginia 25301

or purchased in bookstores throughout West Virginia

ISBN 0-9646197-6-8

INTRODUCTION

Each person expresses his or her feelings for a subject in various ways. Many fine writers have detailed the history of West Virginia through the events of years past, while others have published elegant prose. John Denver's song "Take Me Home, Country Roads" gives a lyrical feeling of the state. My expressions and feelings for West Virginia have been through my photography.

The pages of *A PORTRAIT OF WEST VIRGINIA* journey through the state, with photo images of every region. The photographs are the result of many miles and numerous trips throughout the state.

Having served a tour of duty as a U.S. Army photographer in Germany during the 1960s, I returned home eager to start a career in photography. Young and full of dreams, I headed for New York City where many successful photographers have launched their careers. After a short time in the city, I realized I had left one of the best studios in the world: natural light, mountain beauty, wild flowers and friendly folks—West Virginia.

Back home, Ed Johnson asked me to join the staff of *WONDERFUL WEST VIRGINIA* as the staff photographer. The magazine was in its infancy, and just starting to use color photographs. Ed liked large color transparencies, and with this in mind I sold my prize 35 mm to buy a large 4×5″ Linholf camera with accompanying film holders, lens and tripod, all weighing 35 lbs. This camera was shiny, and the pride of any scenic photographer. I still own and use it, but the shine is gone, much of the covering worn away, the gears are loose; but it still keeps on clicking.

Throughout my professional years, I have been asked about my techniques. My pictures, for the most part, are straightforward photography without filters or devices to alter scenes. Many of the photographs were taken with the camera mounted on a tripod, to allow the use of slow shutter speeds. Also swings and tilts were used, a means of altering the plane of the lens and film in a series of angles to the subject, which gains greater depth of field in the picture. Often slow shutter speeds account for waterfalls to appear as molten steel. I use all focal lengths of lens, wide angles

to telephotos—often photographing a particular scene with several lengths of lens, creating various effects. Lighting at different times of the day creates moods that I find important to the picture. Early morning light is soft, and often there is a mist of fog, which creates a surrealist appearance. Late afternoon light is warm and casts long shadows, giving dimension to a scene. However, the state terrain of hills and valleys often being so close together, shadows are created, which record dark in the photograph giving little detail. I try to avoid noon lighting, since it often appears flat and void of dimension.

I use either Ektachrome or Fugichrome film, since the reproduction is best from the chromes or transparencies in the four-color printing process used in this book.

Some of my most enjoyable photo trips have been simply driving back roads with no intended destination. Finding a scene is like looking for a treasure, then choosing the right lens, film angle and waiting for the right light; a combination of all the elements to make a pleasing photograph. Perhaps one slight drawback to photographing the state is the lack of clear days, especially in the summer. This seems to be characteristic of the weather in the Appalachians. Watching the weather maps for cold fronts, and being ready to go are secrets to catching a clear day.

I became the photographer for *WONDERFUL WEST VIRGINIA* magazine in 1969, and in 1982, upon Ed's retirement, I became editor. This successful publication has become one of the nation's leading state magazines.

Eight years ago I published the first coffee-table-size pictorial book on the state titled *WEST VIRGINIA* which was based on the four seasons of the state. The format of *A PORTRAIT OF WEST VIRGINIA* features the different regions of the state and divides it into northern, western, central, southern and eastern. How to separate the state that is very much county-oriented presented a problem. I asked opinions of many people as to how they would assign a particular county to one of the designated areas. By a general consensus the state shaped up based on my own literary

WHITEWATER RAFTING ON THE LOWER NEW RIVER.

MODEL JACQUELINE STALNAKER TAKES TIME OUT
TO POSE ON THE CANAAN VALLEY SKI SLOPES.

license and not scholastically accepted fact.

Traveling through the state has given me the opportunity to observe both the subtle and obvious differences from region to region. West Virginia is uniquely varied, not only the geographical features, but the people themselves. The personality of the state is tied to the mountains. For instance, take the mountains in the West, which are grand, but are often viewed from afar, perhaps almost untouchable. But here at home the hills are compressed; we live in the hollows, valleys and on the ridges. In essence, we are much more part of the land. Perhaps this closeness extends to families and neighbors, where relationships and values are more appreciated than in mainstream America. As an illustration in point, West Virginia consistently has the lowest crime rate in the nation.

An example of this honesty happened while I was photographing a country church and cemetery. A card company had loaned me a suitcase of valuable Hasselblad cameras and lens to photograph West Virginia and surrounding states for posters and stationery cards. Several hours after photographing the church, I realized I had left the camera and case at the church. I returned there, never expecting to find the equipment since numerous people were about. Ironically, the camera case was still standing at the edge of the cemetery. The case was the size of some of the tombstones, and with the sunlight behind the horizon, it appeared just another tombstone. On any account either no one saw it or—and this is what I believe—the honesty of those folks left it there, knowing the photographer would return.

Over the years as a photographer for the state I've observed changes, some good and some disappointing. However, I've always tried to show the positive side of West Virginia in my pictures. Years ago I photographed Jon Dragon's three rafts, starting the first commercial whitewater trips down the New River. Today up to 1000 people travel down the New River in any one particular day, viewing the beauty of this rugged Gorge, without hurting the environment. While it's fortunate so many people can enjoy the river, the time is past when you could run the river without seeing another soul.

Slowly disappearing are some of the wonderful colloquialisms of speech in the rural parts of the state. I remember stopping in an old country store in Grant County some twenty years ago asking for directions to a scenic spot. A customer asked the store owner, "How did Widow Smith winter?" The reply, "Not worth a durn, found her dead this morning." The store's gone, and perhaps the expression "to winter," implying how well you survived the winter, is lost in time. Also I remember my first ski assignment, holding the ski toe rope with one hand and balancing my camera with the other while going up cabin mountain. Now what luxury, just riding up the mountain on a triple chair lift!

I, like many other photographers in the field, have had dozens of interesting events occur, but I would rather tell the story of West Virginia through the following photos of this book. It is my sincere desire that as the reader journeys through this book, he or she will appreciate the natural beauty God has given West Virginia, and also the beauty man has imparted through his handiwork, be it a quaint building, a fair expressing the heritage of the past, or perhaps a parade in a small West Virginia town.

I would like to acknowledge the people who helped me with this book. First, my lovely wife, Teresa, and daughter Lucia Katherine, who shared and encouraged me throughout all phases of this book. My Mother and Father who so generously gave me support and advice. Martha Mahlie, of Watkins Printing Company, to whom I am truly indebted for her expertise in correcting the copy. Don Smith of Alderson-Broaddus College, whose advice changed the book for the better, and whose counsel I have always valued. My good friend, Mary Hamm, at Oglebay Park, Wheeling, who has always helped me with information and arrangements to obtain photographs in that part of the state. And to all West Virginians and friends who have supported me through *WONDERFUL WEST VIRGINIA* magazine and my other publications. Thank you and God Bless!

Overleaf—HOT AIR BALLOONS FLOAT OVER
THE COUNTRYSIDE NEAR MORGANTOWN, DURING
THE MOUNTAINEER BALLOON FESTIVAL.

NORTHERN

A PART OF THIS REGION is popularly known as the Northern Panhandle. The Ohio River marks one of the boundaries of this area, bordered to the west by the state of Ohio, and to the east and north by Pennsylvania. Influenced by a once flourishing steel industry from these surrounding states, industrial towns emerged along the banks of the Ohio River. Inward, the land is a region of rolling hills with small communities, small farms and remnants of past and present oil wells and coal mines. Weirton, Burning Springs, Mannington, Farmington and Bethlehem are all names synonymous with industries that have played an integral part in the development of this section of the state.

Long before the steel industry, a great mystic culture flourished here and left a legacy of hundreds of earthen burial mounds, moats, and earthen walls. This Adena culture and its Hopewillian and Mississippian successors occupied the region from approximately 1000 B.C. to 700 A.D. Unfortunately, little is left of these earthen structures, except for one outstanding example—Grave Creek Mound at Moundsville, the largest burial mound east of the Mississippi River.

Some years later, another tribe of Indians killed a group of white travelers along the Ohio River and placed their heads on poles as a warning to others. The name of that location, which is now modern day Wheeling, is derived from an Indian word meaning skull. Although an ominous beginning, Wheeling, a modern city, has fine, old Victorian homes; the once largest suspension bridge in the nation; Jamboree USA, second oldest live country music program; and one of the larger municipal parks in the country, Oglebay Park. Just north of Wheeling, Weirton is the home of Weirton Steel Corporation, which is a national success story. A few years ago the employees bought out the struggling company and turned it into a prosperous steel producer for America. Outside of Weirton on Kings Creek Road, Peter Tarr's Iron Furnace was the first blast furnace west of the Alleghenies, built in 1794. This furnace cast the cannon balls used by Commodore Perry's fleet during the Battle of Lake Erie.

Fifty miles southeast of Wheeling, at Morgantown, West Virginia University, the first university in the state, was founded in 1867. Both West Virginia and Marshall Universities engendered an unusually high level of pride throughout West Virginia by their 1988 successful football season. Though less heralded, academic achievements, as evidenced by the number of Rhodes scholars and other honors awarded each year, are of equal pride to the state.

Prior to the Civil War era, nighttime illumination was largely dependent on the use of candles and whale oil. These were smelly, expensive and unsatisfactory. Attention was soon focused on petroleum as a better fuel. West Virginia petroleum seeps (oil oozing above ground) had been known about since early times.

Shallow wells were drilled by methods we would now consider primitive, but they did produce relatively large quantities of oil. West Virginia became the world's major producer for a time. This bonanza created a lively lease-land speculation and population boom in the producing areas. As an example, the town of Burning Springs had a 300 percent increase in population almost overnight.

Production from shallow wells soon decreased significantly when new drilling techniques were developed which allowed tapping the deep rock strata. Although West Virginia still has a healthy oil and gas industry, it is no longer dominant.

Memories of the state's early boom days are kept alive by the Oil and Gas Festival held in the beautiful town of Sistersville each September. Also, the many abandoned derricks and pumping devices dotting the rural countryside are landmarks of boom times in the past.

Each era of history has left a visible impact on the area: burial mounds, oil and gas wells and the more recent coal and steel industries.

THE OHIO RIVER, LOOKING NORTHEAST, WITH TYLER COUNTY ON THE RIGHT AND THE STATE OF OHIO ON THE LEFT.

Top—PETER TARR'S IRON FURNACE, THE FIRST BLAST FURNACE WEST OF THE ALLEGHENIES, BUILT IN 1794. THE FURNACE IS LOCATED IN HANCOCK COUNTY. *Right*—RECREATIONAL LAKE AT TOMLINSON RUN STATE PARK IN HANCOCK COUNTY. *Below*—STEAM AND NIGHTTIME ENSHROUD THE WEIRTON STEEL CORPORATION PLANT.

Top—BROOKE COUNTY COURTHOUSE AREA AT WELLSBURG. *Above*—VIEW OF THE OHIO RIVER FROM THE CITY OF WELLSBURG. *Left*—COMMENCEMENT HALL AT BETHANY COLLEGE, ONE OF THE EARLIEST AND BEST EXAMPLES OF COLLEGIATE ARCHITECTURE IN THE UNITED STATES.

EVENING SCENE OF HISTORIC SUSPENSION BRIDGE AT WHEELING IN DECEMBER 1987. DECORATIVE LIGHTING WAS ADDED, EVOKING THE SPIRIT OF PAST ATTEMPTS TO LIGHT THE SPAN IN THE MID-1800S.

OGLEBAY MANSION LOCATED AT OGLEBAY PARK, NORTH OF WHEELING, ONE OF THE LARGEST
MUNICIPAL PARKS IN THE UNITED STATES.

SPRING FLOWERS USHER IN SPRING ALONG FISHING CREEK IN WETZEL COUNTY.

EVENING SUN SILHOUETTES GRAVE CREEK MOUND, THE LARGEST ADENA BURIAL MOUND EAST
OF THE MISSISSIPPI RIVER. A PREHISTORIC ADENA CULTURE WHICH BUILT THIS EARTH STRUC-
TURE LIVED IN THE AREA FROM ABOUT 1000 B.C. TO APPROXIMATELY 700 A.D. GRAVE CREEK
MOUND STATE PARK IS LOCATED IN MOUNDSVILLE.

Top—SCENE ALONG THE OHIO RIVER AT SISTERSVILLE. *Left*—MRS. RICHARD ARMOR (MISS POM POM) CLOWNS DURING THE PARADE AT THE OIL GAS FESTIVAL, RELIVING THE OIL BOOM DAYS OF THE 1890S. *Below*—OIL CANS ILLUSTRATE THE HISTORIC OIL INDUSTRY IN TYLER COUNTY.

Above—DIESEL ENGINE PULLS A LONG STRING OF COAL CARS PAST HISTORIC B&O TERMINAL AT GRAFTON DURING THE EARLY MORNING HOURS. *Left*—AERIAL VIEW OF VALLEY FALLS STATE PARK ON THE TYGART RIVER BETWEEN FAIRMONT AND GRAFTON.

Top—HOT AIR BALLOONS BEGIN ASCENSION AT HART FIELD, MORGANTOWN, DURING THE MOUNTAINEER BALLOON FESTIVAL. *Above*—AERIAL VIEW OF WEST VIRGINIA UNIVERSITY'S STADIUM, HOME OF THE OUTSTANDING WV MOUNTAINEER FOOTBALL TEAM. *Right*—WOODBURN CIRCLE AT WEST VIRGINIA UNIVERSITY, MORGANTOWN, WHERE UNIVERSITY BEGAN IN THE STATE IN 1867.

A FAVORITE FISHING HOLE BELOW BRUCETON MILLS, ON THE BIG SANDY CREEK IN PRESTON COUNTY.

A WINTER DAY IN CATHEDRAL STATE FOREST, EAST OF AURORA. THIS 133 ACRES OF VIRGIN TIMBER IS TYPICAL OF HOW THE FORESTS OF THE STATE LOOKED BEFORE THE TURN-OF-THE-CENTURY TIMBERING.

Above—THE NATIONAL CEMETERY AT GRAFTON OFFERS MUTE TESTIMONY TO AMERICA'S BRAVE WHO SACRIFICED FOR THEIR COUNTRY. *Right*—A MIST SURROUNDS TREES AT TYGART LAKE STATE PARK.

MUSKET FIRE ECHOES THROUGH THE HILLS AT PRICKETTS FORT NEAR FAIRMONT. THE RECON-
STRUCTED FORT RECREATES LIFE OF THE LATE 18TH CENTURY IN COLONIAL WESTERN VIRGINIA,
AS A REFUGE FROM INDIAN ATTACKS. THE ORIGINAL FORT WAS BUILT IN 1774.

IF BORN A CENTURY OR TWO EARLIER, ERIN GRACE WILSON AND TWINS ANTHEA LEA AND BRANDY RANAI WILSON WOULD HAVE LOOKED MUCH THE PART OF THE PRICKETTS FORT AREA.

WESTERN

THE AREA DESIGNATED AS WESTERN has a number of interesting aspects that lend local color. A girl's hands form a piece of pottery with clay on the potter's wheel at the Mountain State Art and Craft Fair. An elderly lady graciously explains the workings of early farming in the West Virginia State Farm Museum. From a fiery furnace, a gatherer takes a portion of molten glass and gives it to a finisher who fashions a beautiful piece of glassware. The plop-plop of a boat paddle wheel plies itself through the waters of the broad Ohio River carrying passengers to historic Blennerhassett Island.

These scenes typify this region of the state: a land of rolling hills, with many broad and fertile valleys, rich in farms and river life; this part of the state has its roots inherently tied to its river towns such as St. Marys, Parkersburg, Ravenswood, Point Pleasant, Huntington; and its rural county seats of Wayne, Hamlin, Winfield, Ripley, Elizabeth and Harrisville.

When traveling through this area, a feeling of the heritage of the region can be experienced by visiting various attractions. The Mountain State Art and Craft Fair held annually at Cedar Lakes as a 4th of July celebration, is one of West Virginia's major attractions where artists make, exhibit and sell a wide range of handcrafted items.

The handblown glass industry had an early beginning in West Virginia, due to an abundance of raw materials such as natural gas and pure silica sand. The artistry of glassmaking can be observed at such plants as Fenton Glass Company at Williamstown and Blenko Glass Company at Milton.

The West Virginia State Farm Museum near Point Pleasant consists of 31 buildings, each providing a glimpse into the life of early farm families.

Blennerhassett Island Historical Park on the Ohio River near Parkersburg, was the site where Aaron Burr and Harman Blennerhassett allegedly conceived a plan in 1806 to overthrow the Unived States Government. The Blennerhassett Mansion has been faithfully reconstructed and is used each August to present a musical drama, "Eden of the River," portraying events of the island's history.

The city of Huntington is one of West Virginia's most important industrial, commercial and cultural areas. The beautiful campus of Marshall University is in the confines of the city. A restored B&O railroad station, named Heritage Village, offers food and railroad lore. The street system of Huntington was laid out in an orderly survey in 1870, and still adheres to this plan.

Numerous opportunities for hunting, fishing, boating, camping and other recreational pursuits abound. Special public lands have been set aside for just such purposes. They are McClintic Wildlife Station near Point Pleasant, Chief Cornstalk Public Hunting Area near the Kanawha River in Mason County, Mill Creek Public Hunting Area in Cabell County, Hilbert and Big Ugly Public Hunting and Fishing Areas in Lincoln County. Two large lakes in Wayne County, Beech Fork and East Lynn Lake, offer boating, fishing and hunting. Cabwaylingo State Forest in Wayne County is another excellent choice for recreation.

In 1753, George Washington claimed 200,000 acres in this approximate region and called it Augusta. France and England once waged war over these fertile lands. It is known from archaeological studies and recorded history that the Kanawha and Ohio rivers, plus numerous smaller streams, played a major role in the lives of people who chose to live in these vicinities. The early people depended on the rivers primarily for food and transportation, while in recent times river traffic has lured a wide variety of industries. Today the land is blessed with rich heritage and fine people.

HISTORIC COVERED BRIDGE AT CEDAR LAKES CONFERENCE CENTER AND FFA-FHA CAMP NEAR RIPLEY.

Top—SCENE INSIDE THE FENTON ART GLASS COMPANY PLANT AT WILLIAMSTOWN. *Right*—A BOAT PADDLE WHEEL LEAVES A WAKE ON THE OHIO RIVER, WITH BLENNERHASSETT ISLAND IN THE BACKGROUND. *Below*—A HANDLER ATTACHES A GLOWING RIBBON OF GLASS, FORMING A HANDLE ON A BASKET, AT FENTON ART GLASS COMPANY.

Above—AN AUTUMN FARM SCENE NEAR GRIFFITHSVILLE IN LINCOLN COUNTY. *Right*—WINTER STORM BLANKETS FARMLAND NEAR CARIO IN RITCHIE COUNTY.

EARLY AUTUMN ALONG THE NORTH FORK OF THE HUGHES RIVER IN NORTH BEND STATE PARK.

A FRIENDLY GAME OF FOOTBALL TAKES PLACE IN FRONT OF THE WIRT COUNTY COURTHOUSE
AT ELIZABETH. *Overleaf*—REFLECTIONS OF FALL IN A SMALL STREAM IN PLEASANT COUNTY.

Top—MOUNTAIN STATE ART AND CRAFT FAIR SEEN FROM ABOVE AT CEDAR LAKES. *Left*—APPRENTICE KATIE DANIELS FASHIONS A PIECE ON THE POTTERS WHEEL DURING THE MOUNTAIN STATE ARTS AND CRAFTS FAIR. *Below*—AUTUMN LANDSCAPE IN JACKSON COUNTY.

FIELD OF FLOWERS NEAR FRAZIERS BOTTOM, SEEN FROM ROUTE 35 IN PUTMAN COUNTY.

BUFFALO PRESBYTERIAN CHURCH, ESTABLISHED 1857, AT BUFFALO. THE ADJACENT BUILDING, NOW VACANT, FORMERLY HOUSED BUFFALO ACADEMY, WHICH WAS ESTABLISHED IN 1849.

HOME OF GENERAL JOHN McCAUSLAND, 1837–1927, WHO WAS ONE OF THE OFFICERS OF THE
GENERAL STAFF OF THE CONFEDERATE ARMY. THIS HOME IS LOCATED ON ROUTE 35 IN MASON
COUNTY.

MILDRED HARGRAVES OF POINT PLEASANT GRACIOUSLY EXPLAINS THE HISTORIC ITEMS AND
SPECIAL EVENTS AT THE WEST VIRGINIA STATE FARM MUSEUM LOCATED FOUR MILES NORTH OF
POINT PLEASANT.

OHIO RIVER SEEN FROM THE STATE OF OHIO RIVERBANKS LOOKING TOWARD PLEASANT COUNTY.

THE ORIGINAL OLD MAIN, THE REVERED WEST-END SECTION KNOWN AS THE "TOWERS," GRACES
THE CAMPUS OF MARSHALL UNIVERSITY AT HUNTINGTON.

Top—AERIAL VIEW OF HUNTINGTON, HOME OF MARSHALL UNIVERSITY. *Right*—LOFTY CANOPY OF TREE LIMBS SHELTERS SIDEWALK DURING WINTER AT RITTER PARK IN HUNTINGTON. *Below*— EAST HUNTINGTON BRIDGE, COMPLETED IN 1985, LINKS OHIO AND WEST VIRGINIA.

A PORTION OF EAST LYNN LAKE IN WAYNE COUNTY SEEN FROM THE AIR. THE LAKE WAS DESIGNED
BY THE U.S. ARMY CORPS OF ENGINEERS.

AERIAL VIEW OF WAYNE, COUNTY SEAT OF WAYNE COUNTY. WAYNE WAS FIRST INCORPORATED
AS FAIRVIEW IN 1882, AND THE NAME LATER CHANGED TO WAYNE IN 1911.

CENTRAL

ONE EXCELLENT WAY TO SEE and get a feel for the central region of the state is to drive up Interstate 79 from Charleston to Clarksburg on an early summer morning. The rolling countryside bordering the interstate has fields and forests of poplars and oaks. Sycamores with stark white trunks grow along the numerous creek banks throughout these areas. Chances are a fog will blanket the road, with the early morning sun burning away the mist as the morning wears on.

By turning off any of the exits along the interstate, one can find appreciation of West Virginia's heartland. Going either east or west, two lane roads wind through hills, valleys, quaint towns and small farms that blend into the countryside.

A few miles off the interstate, the town of Spencer each autumn features the Black Walnut Festival. A festival so typical of an American tradition: parades, high school bands, exhibits, hot dogs and Cokes.

Close by in Calhoun County, an unusual eight-sided church can be found; this is only one of the numerous churches that adorn the landscape.

Turning off the Flatwoods Exit and going north, a bit of the Irish can be seen and heard in the small town of Ireland. Bagpipes might be heard celebrating St. Patrick's Day, and a four-leaf clover surely can be found.

Continuing north, French Creek Game Farm provides an interesting stop to observe West Virginia's wildlife. This 329-acre wildlife preserve has fifty different kinds of wildlife native to the state—even a few species that disappeared a few hundred or so years ago, such as buffalo, elk and timber wolves.

Near the town of Jane Lew is Jackson's Mill, the site of the boyhood home of General "Stonewall" Jackson. The grist mill's waterwheel is unique in that it operates horizontally, instead of in the traditional vertical manner.

Throughout the region, covered bridges have been preserved as a heritage of the past. One of the most famous is at Philippi, which was the scene of the first Civil War land battle.

Clarksburg hosts the Italian Heritage Festival each year, with the streets being transformed to a Renaissance Italy. Music, Italian foods, dancing, an organ grinder and a Sunday Catholic Mass Celebration on the main street highlight the festival.

These are just a small number of the areas of interest throughout central West Virginia.

Perhaps a broader view of the region can be obtained by flying over the countryside. The terrain, for the most part, is a pattern of rolling hills and valleys, often with little sense of direction. Many of the valleys have a road ending at the end of the hollow, with a lonely-looking house and barn. Viewed through the four seasons, the hills project a barrenness during winter. Come spring and summer, a carpet of green foliage blankets the countryside. During autumn the hills are transformed into a multitude of oranges and reds.

If the flight were to pass over Charleston, the view of the West Virginia Capitol complex could be considered one of the most beautiful in the country. The recently completed gold dome adds further distinction, particularly when the afternoon sun reflects off it.

Charleston seen from the air is nestled in a valley with the Kanawha River as a highlight. Historically, the city has been a leader in establishing churches, schools, and various literary and cultural endeavors.

This is a region of many events and attractions. Exploring the countryside is a rewarding adventure, especially meeting the many fine people who make this their home.

A RED BARN CONTRASTS WITH FRESHLY FALLEN SNOW IN RURAL BRAXTON COUNTY.

WINDING ROAD THROUGH WATTERS SMITH MEMORIAL STATE PARK ADDS RUSTIC CHARM TO THIS AUTUMN SCENE.

SIMPSON CREEK COVERED BRIDGE, LOCATED AT BRIDGEPORT. THE BRIDGE WAS NAMED FOR
JOHN SIMPSON, A WELL-KNOWN PEDDLER AND INDIAN TRADER.

WINTER SNOWFALL BLANKETS A FARM IN RURAL BARBOUR COUNTY NEAR CENTURY.

AN EARLY SPRING SNOW ADDS BEAUTY TO SCENIC BIRCH RIVER NEAR HEROLD IN BRAXTON COUNTY.

Above—THE SMALL COMMUNITY OF IRELAND IN LEWIS COUNTY IS MADE UP OF IRISH DESCEND-ANTS. *Right*—EARLY MORNING SUN CASTS A GOLDEN HUE ON MIDDLE FORK RIVER AS IT FLOWS THROUGH AUDRA STATE PARK.

IN 1761 JOHN AND SAMUEL PRINGEL (BROTHERS) SETTLED IN THE BUCKHANNON AREA USING
A LARGE CAVITY IN A SYCAMORE TREE AS A HOME. THE SECOND GROWTH OF THIS TREE IS
MEMORIALIZED BY A SMALL PARK NORTH OF BUCKHANNON, ON THE BUCKHANNON RIVER.

Top—AN ELK AT FRENCH CREEK GAME FARM. THIS 329-ACRE WILDLIFE PRESERVE, 12 MILES SOUTH OF BUCKHANNON, HAS OVER FIFTY DIFFERENT KINDS OF WILDLIFE NATIVE TO WEST VIRGINIA. *Above*—WEST UNION, COUNTY SEAT OF DODDRIDGE COUNTY.

Above—SUMMER SHOWERS DOT THE SURFACE OF THE FISHING PONDS AT CEDAR CREEK STATE PARK IN GILMER COUNTY. *Right*—AERIAL VIEW OF FARMLAND DURING SPRING NEAR FLATWOODS.

THE CHUTE CREATED BY WATER EROSION OVER THOUSANDS OF YEARS ON FALL RUN IN WEBSTER COUNTY.

UPPER FALLS ON FALL RUN IN HOLLY RIVER STATE PARK DURING THE AUTUMN SEASON.

Top—CIVIL WAR REENACTMENT AT CARNIFEX FERRY BATTLEFIELD STATE PARK. *Above*—CRANBERRY RIVER AT WOODBINE RECREATION AREA IN THE MONONGAHELA NATIONAL FOREST. *Left*—ENON CHURCH IN NICHOLAS COUNTY.

FOREBODING CLOUDS GRACE THE HORIZON IN A REMOTE AREA OF CLAY COUNTY.

CLAY COUNTY HAS THE DISTINCTION OF HAVING HAD THREE COURTHOUSES. THE YELLOW COURTHOUSE WAS THE SECOND, WHILE THE THIRD IS A CONTEMPORARY BUILDING DIRECTLY ACROSS THE STREET.

Top—EARLY MORNING DAWN CASTS A GOLDEN HUE OVER CHARLESTON. *Left*—FIREWORKS ADD COLOR TO THE STERNWHEEL REGATTA IN CHARLESTON. *Below*—AERIAL VIEW OF THE STATE CAPITOL COMPLEX IN CHARLESTON.

Top—MAJORETTES PARADE THROUGH THE STREETS OF SPENCER DURING THE BLACK WALNUT FESTIVAL. *Above*—FALL OFFERS MANY BEAUTIFUL FARM SCENES IN ROANE COUNTY.

Above—THE TOWN OF SPENCER HOSTS BANDS FROM SURROUNDING COUNTIES DURING THE BLACK WALNUT FESTIVAL. *Overleaf*—EARLY MORNING LIGHT RAYS IN WEBSTER COUNTY.

ALBERT'S CHAPEL, UNITED METHODIST CHURCH, IS A UNIQUE 8-SIDED CHURCH IN CALHOUN COUNTY.

JACKSON'S MILL 4-H CAMP, 5 MILES NORTH OF WESTON ON U.S. 19. THE MILL IS THE SITE OF THE BOYHOOD HOME OF GENERAL "STONEWALL" JACKSON.

SOUTHERN

MILLIONS OF YEARS AGO in geological time, seas and great swamps covered the region depositing horizontal beds of limestone, sandstone and shale. Starting some 300 million years past, densely forested swamps with luxuriant tree ferns, horsetails, giant club mosses and fern-like plants covered the land. The dead plants from these forests decayed, and formed the first step of the formation of coal called peat. As the years passed, sediment was deposited over these layers of peat producing heat and pressure to transform the mass to a compressed organic black rock-like material which is now mined throughout the state. This land mass was uplifted high above the sea level creating the Appalachian Plateau. Streams and wind eroded the plateau, until today we have rugged forested mountains and valleys with numerous creeks, waterfalls and whitewater rivers.

The Paleo-Indian first inhabited the area about 13,000 B.C., followed by many tribes: Adena, Armstrong, Buck Garden, Fort Ancient, Cherokee, Shawnee, Delaware and Seneca. Perhaps even mysterious visitors came before Columbus. Rock carvings (petroglyphs) with an ancient language exist on cliffs throughout southern West Virginia. Some of the first pioneer settlers to arrive were families given 1000 acres by the government of Virginia in 1745. This land was in the Greenbrier Valley. With the influx of settlers, churches, small communities, and grist mills graced the countryside.

Following the Civil War, migrant workers came seeking employment with a new emerging coal and timbering industry. These sturdy and proud people created a historic coal era: unions, coal barons, mine wars. "The Hatfields and McCoys" famous feud in the late nineteenth century became well known.

When Franklin D. Roosevelt became president in 1933, a depression gripped the nation. He established the Civilian Conservation Corps, known as the CCC. The CCC helped save America's lands and forests, and gave training and employment to young men through conservation projects.

Throughout southern West Virginia, excellent examples of this work are evident. In the older state parks and forests, many of the cabins, administration buildings, picnic shelters, roads and stone structures are testimony to these past conservation works. One notable example is Camp Washington Carver in Fayette County.

One of the legacies of the CCC works often overlooked is the quality of individuality. No two fireplaces are exactly the same in the state park cabins. Even the blacksmith made latches on each door differ.

A region diverse in itself offers much. Organized whitewater rafting on the New and Gauley rivers with superb rapids and scenery, affording glimpses of ghost mining towns. Famous resorts such as the Greenbrier, state park resorts as Pipestem and Twin Falls welcome guests from around the world. The history of the region is relived each summer night through outdoor dramas: "Honey in the Rock" and "Hatfields and McCoys" in Grandview State Park and "The Aracoma Story" at Chief Logan State Park.

Historically, southern West Virginians are like her terrain, rugged and proud people who have tenaciously clung to a way of life quite unique.

COLORFUL FALL FOLIAGE ENHANCES THE PICTURESQUE OLD MILL AT BABCOCK STATE PARK.

Above —RAFTERS PLOW THROUGH A RAPID ON THE MIGHTY GAULEY RIVER, ONE OF THE TOP TEN WHITEWATER RIVERS IN THE WORLD. THE GAULEY RIVER MAKES UP PART OF THE NEW RIVER GORGE NATIONAL RIVER. *Right* —SANDSTONE FALLS ON THE NEW RIVER, NORTH OF HINTON, IS IN THE NEW RIVER GORGE NATIONAL RIVER.

COUNTRY ROAD LEADS TO RESTORED PIONEER FARM AT TWIN FALLS STATE PARK, IN WYOMING COUNTY.

AERIAL VIEW OF TAMARACK, THE FINEST ARTS AND CRAFT CENTER IN THE UNITED STATES, IS LOCATED OFF THE WEST VIRGINIA TURNPIKE AT BECKLEY.

Top—AN UNUSUAL PETROGLYPH IN A ROCK SHELTER NEAR OCEANA, THOUGHT BY SOME AR-
CHAEOLOGISTS AND LINGUISTS TO BE AN ANCIENT IRISH LANGUAGE CALLED OGAM WITH A
CHRISTIAN MESSAGE. *Above*—LAUREL LAKE PUBLIC HUNTING AND FISHING AREA IN MINGO
COUNTY.

Top—A BUTTERFLY IN MOTION AMONG FLOWERS ON A HILLSIDE IN SUMMERS COUNTY. *Above*—A VIEW OF BLUESTONE GORGE FROM PIPESTEM STATE PARK. *Overleaf*—DOUBLE RAINBOW GRACES OLD WHITE AT THE FAMOUS GREENBRIER RESORT. AN EVENING SUN GIVES A GOLDEN HUE SIMILAR TO A RENAISSANCE PAINTING.

Top—SCENE FROM THE PLAY "HATFIELDS AND McCOYS." *Left*—THE HATFIELD FAMILY CEMETERY AT SARAH ANN IN LOGAN COUNTY. LIFE-SIZE STATUE OF DEVIL ANSE WAS ERECTED IN 1922. *Below*—AERIAL VIEW OF THE RUGGED TERRAIN IN MINGO COUNTY WHERE SOME OF THE FEUD TOOK PLACE.

Above—LATE SUMMER FLOWERS ADORN A SMALL STREAM IN MERCER COUNTY. *Left*—A SPRING VIEW OF BRUSH CREEK FALLS IN MERCER COUNTY.

Above—CAMP WASHINGTON CARVER BUILT BY THE CIVILIAN CONSERVATION CORPS IN FAYETTE COUNTY. IT WAS OPERATED AS A 4-H CAMP FOR BLACK CHILDREN BY WEST VIRGINIA STATE COLLEGE INSTITUTE, DURING 1942–45. *Right*—AUTUMN VIEW OF NEW RIVER FROM HAWKS NEST STATE PARK.

A SCENE OF PINNACLE ROCK NEAR JULIAN IN BOONE COUNTY, WHICH HAS HISTORIC INDIAN CARVINGS.

Top—HOBET MINING COMPLEX ACROSS FROM ROUTE 119 IN BOONE COUNTY. *Above*—EVENING VIEW OF DANVILLE.

VIEW LOOKING TOWARD THE NEW RIVER FROM SANDSTONE IN RALEIGH COUNTY, WITH A COAL MINE TIPPLE IN THE BACKGROUND.

MOUNTAIN RANGE NORTH OF BLUE BEND IN GREENBRIER COUNTY.

EVENING SUN CASTS LONG SHADOWS AMONG THE HILLS AT ELKHORN IN McDOWELL COUNTY
IN THE SOUTHERN PART OF THE STATE.

THE FRONT DOOR TO THE EXQUISITELY CONSTRUCTED BANK AT BRAMWELL, THE TOWN OF
NUMEROUS FORMER MILLIONAIRES AND LUXURIOUS HOMES, DURING THE GOLDEN ERA OF THE
COAL MINING INDUSTRY.

ATHENS LAKE OWNED BY THE CITY OF ATHENS AS A WATER SUPPLY. THIS LAKE OF 27 ACRES OFFERS FINE FISHING TO THE REGION.

SUNSET ALONG A LONELY STRETCH OF ROAD IN MONROE COUNTY NEAR WAITEVILLE.

EASTERN

THE FATHER OF OUR COUNTRY, George Washington, once considered establishing our nation's capital at Shepherdstown, one of the oldest towns in the state. Thomas Shepherd settled the town Mecklenburg in 1762. In 1798 it was renamed Shepherdstown in his honor, and became the location for James Rumsey's first successful steamboat. A few miles south and some years later, an obsessed man climbed the stairs to meet the hangman's noose at Charles Town on December 2, 1859. John Brown's famous raid to secure arms at Harpers Ferry Federal Arsenal was a major historical event that helped precipitate the Civil War.

The Potomac and Shenandoah Rivers flow past Harpers Ferry and mirror the images of an American National Historical Park in the Eastern Panhandle. History of the region is emphasized by names such as Bunker Hill, Suit Castle, Lee Cabin, Berkeley Springs, Fort Ashby and Nancy Hank's Birthplace. Gracious southern mansions built by George Washington and his brothers are reminders of an elegant way of early life in this part of the state. This vast wilderness yielded millions of board feet of timber for the world. Cass Scenic Railroad, with its gear-driven, steam-powered Shay locomotives still operates as a tourist attraction, providing a glimpse of yesterday's lumbering era. Helvettia is a Swiss village where the ancestral customs, such as making cheese the old way, have changed little over the years.

The topography of this area is referred to as the Allegheny Plateau and Potomac Section, with a succession of parallel mountain ranges. Some of these mountains exceed 4000 feet in height, with Spruce Knob the highest point in the state at 4862 feet. These mountains cradle natural treasures, such as streams that flow under mountains to reappear on the opposite side, caverns, remote wilderness areas, trout streams and beautiful rock formations.

Because of the natural beauty, this region beckons visitors with varying recreational pursuits. Backpackers find Dolly Sods a treasure of 10,000 acres of designated wilderness area, a wind-swept land where the trees are three-sided from the prevailing winds. Otter Creek is another wilderness area of pristine beauty. Spruce Knob, Smokehole Caverns, Bakers Rocks, Greenland Gap and Champe Rocks exemplify the beauty of geological rock formations. The terrain and snow conditions have promoted the building of popular ski resorts.

A number of state parks and forests have guest facilities throughout the region: Blackwater Falls, Holly River, Kumbrabow, Seneca, Canaan Valley, Cacapon are names that lend romance to the settings. Quaint inns and bed-and-breakfast establishments are popular throughout the area.

When man first occupied this region, the sounds of nature could be heard: thunder, animals, the wind rushing through trees. These are still heard today, but a new dimension of sound is now recorded by large metal ears that stand like intruders on the horizon, almost from another world. Radio astronomers at the Radio Astronomy Center at Green Bank listen and interpret signals from outer space.

This vast wilderness region was settled by pioneers of Irish-German descent. Now as in their time the hunting and fishing are excellent, with George Washington and Monongahela National Forests offering thousands of acres of game habitat.

The eastern section of the state with its indigenous natural beauty and historical heritage, offers much to visitors and the people living there.

BLACKWATER FALLS IN
BLACKWATER FALLS
STATE PARK.

Top— ONE OF THE MANY LARGE RADIO TELESCOPES THAT EXPLORES THE UNIVERSE IS LOCATED AT GREEN BANK. *Left*— THE RESTORED RAILROAD STATION AT MARLINGTON. *Below*— EARLY MORNING MIST RISES FROM KELLBUCK AT WATOGA STATE PARK.

LATE SUMMER WILDFLOWERS ADD BEAUTY TO A SMALL STREAM BANK IN HAMPSHIRE COUNTY.

PASTORAL VIEW OF CHAMPE ROCKS ALONG ROUTE 28 NORTH OF SENECA ROCKS.

Top—CHILDREN PERFORM NATIVE DANCES AT HELVETIA, A SMALL TOWN IN RANDOLPH COUNTY SETTLED BY A SWISS COLONY MANY YEARS AGO. *Left*—OLD BARN ADDS TO PICTURESQUE VIEW IN RURAL RANDOLPH COUNTY. *Below*—CATTLE GRAZE IN FRONT OF BAKER ROCKS NEAR MOOREFIELD.

Above—AN ENGLISH NORMAN CASTLE BUILT BY 53-YEAR-OLD COL. SAMUEL TAYLOR SUIT IN 1885 TO ENTICE THE LOVELY YOUNG ROSA PELHAM, DAUGHTER OF AN ALABAMA CONGRESSMAN, TO MARRY HIM. THE TURRETED STONE CASTLE OVERLOOKS BERKELEY SPRINGS. *Right*—AN EERIE ROAD LEADS THROUGH A FOREST IN THE EASTERN PANHANDLE, PERHAPS TO A CASTLE.

Top—HISTORIC TOWN OF THOMAS, AN IMPORTANT LUMBERING TOWN AT THE TURN OF THE CENTURY. *Above*—BLACKWATER RIVER IN CANAAN VALLEY STATE PARK.

BLACKWATER FALLS, IN BLACKWATER FALLS STATE PARK, IS ONE OF WEST VIRGINIA'S MOST NOTED
SCENIC NATURAL ATTRACTIONS.

Above—HOPEVILLE CANYON OF THE NORTH FORK OF THE SOUTH BRANCH OF THE POTOMAC RIVER. *Left*—CLIFFS IN GREENLAND GAP, A NARROW VALLEY NEAR THE COMMUNITY OF SCHERR. THE WEST VIRGINIA CHAPTER OF THE NATURE CONSERVANCY HAS ACQUIRED AND PRESERVED THIS UNIQUE AREA.

PASTORAL VIEW OF PATTERSON CREEK WINDING THROUGH MINERAL COUNTY.

A SCENE FROM DOLLY SODS LOOKING TOWARD PETERSBURG AND MOOREFIELD. *Overleaf*—CANAAN VALLEY SKI RESORT, ONE OF WEST VIRGINIA'S PREMIER SKI FACILITIES.

PROSPECT HILL, ONE OF THE FORMER PLANTATIONS IN THE EASTERN PANHANDLE, LOCATED AT
GERRARDSTOWN. THIS GEORGIAN STYLE MANSION'S NORTH SECTION WAS COMPLETED IN 1792
AND THE SOUTH WING IN 1804. IT NOW SERVES AS A POPULAR BED-AND-BREAKFAST INN.

NIGHT SCENE OF BERKELEY SPRINGS STATE PARK. THE SPA STILL OFFERS ROMAN BATHS AND VARIOUS HEAT TREATMENTS. DURING THE 1800S, MINERAL SPRINGS MADE THE AREA FAMOUS AS A HEALTH RESORT.

EARLY MORNING STREET SCENE IN HISTORIC HARPERS FERRY NATIONAL HISTORICAL PARK, SITE
OF JOHN BROWN'S FAMOUS RAID ON THE UNITED STATES FEDERAL ARSENAL IN 1859.

JEFFERSON COUNTY COURTHOUSE AT CHARLES TOWN, BUILT IN 1837. THIS COURTHOUSE WAS
USED IN JOHN BROWN'S TREASON TRIAL IN 1859.

Top—QUAINT BUILDING ALONG THE MAIN STREET IN SHEPHERDSTOWN, ONE OF THE OLDEST TOWNS IN WEST VIRGINIA. *Right*—TRINITY EPISCOPAL CHURCH, ESTABLISHED IN 1747, WELCOMES VISITORS IN SHEPHERDSTOWN. *Below*—SPRING BEAUTY ALONG A SIDE STREET IN SHEPHERDSTOWN.

THE STATE MOTTO, *Montane Semper Liberi* (TRANSLATED AS, MOUNTAINEERS ARE ALWAYS FREE) MAY BE LIKENED TO THE FREEDOM OF THIS CHILD SKIPPING DOWN A PATH AT PIPE-STEM STATE PARK.